Train to

Written by Samantha Montgomerie

Collins

Sled dogs are big and strong. They have an **instinct** to pull.

This sport is perfect for them. They like training on the trails.

The Arctic is freezing. Storms are bitter.
The **sweeping plains** are steep.

Sled dogs have thick coats to keep out the chill. They train so they can finish the trails.

"All right!" hollers the musher. The dogs run at speed on the trail.

musher

Sled dogs are smart. The musher trains the dogs to hear orders.

The dogs hear the signal to run.
They sprint off down the steep trail.

The dogs set the speed. Swing dogs tug the sled out from trees.

swing dogs

The sled speeds by the markers. The dogs strain harder. They speed off to win.

markers

The sled swoops to the finish.
The crowd claps. The dogs yelp.

Sled dogs train hard. Now they must sleep and wait to run again.

Glossary

instinct born to do it with no thinking

sweeping plains curving flat land

Trail map

Review: After reading

Use your assessment from hearing the children read to choose any GPCs, words or tricky words that need additional practice.

Read 1: Decoding

- Practise reading words ending in "-ing" by blending one chunk of the word at a time:

  train/ing   freez/ing   sweep/ing

- Challenge the children to read the following words ending in "-er", in the same way:

  bitt/er   mush/er   ord/ers

  holl/ers   mark/ers   hard/er

Read 2: Prosody

- Choose two double page spreads and model reading with expression to the children.
- Ask the children to have a go at reading the same pages with expression.
- Reread the whole book to the children to model fluency and rhythm in the story.

Read 3: Comprehension

- Turn to pages 14 and 15 and encourage the children to use the photos to describe what the musher and dogs are doing at each place during the race.
- For every question ask the children how they know the answer. Ask:
  o Why must the dogs be able to hear well? (e.g. *they need to be able to hear the musher's shouts*)
  o Return to page 10. Why do you think there are markers? (e.g. *to show which way to go through the snow*)
  o Why are the dogs good sled-pullers? (e.g. *they are strong, have thick coats and are clever*)
  o What have you learnt about sled races?